FRIENDLY REMINDERS

LESSONS FROM A SELF-CARE SAVAGE

SCOTT TATUM

ROCK
POINT

First published in 2023 by Rock Point,
an imprint of The Quarto Group,
142 West 36th Street, 4th Floor,
New York, NY 10018, USA
T (212) 779-4972 F (212) 779-6058
www.Quarto.com

Rock Point titles are also available at discount
for retail, wholesale, promotional, and bulk
purchase. For details, contact the Special Sales
Manager by email at specialsales@quarto.com
or by mail at The Quarto Group, Attn: Special
Sales Manager, 100 Cummings Center Suite
265D, Beverly, MA 01915 USA.

10 9 8 7 6 5 4 3

ISBN: 978-1-63106-933-8

Library of Congress Control Number:
2023933264

Publisher: Rage Kindelsperger
Editorial Director: Erin Canning
Creative Director: Laura Drew
Senior Art Director: Marisa Kwek
Managing Editor: Cara Donaldson
Editor: Keyla Pizarro-Hernández
Cover and Interior Design: Abi Read

Printed in the USA

TO MY BEAUTIFUL SONS, JACOB AND BEN,
MY WHYS THAT KEEP ME FULL OF PURPOSE
AND FOCUSED ON WHAT IS IMPORTANT IN LIFE.

I SELF-CARE SAVAGE UP TO BE BETTER EVERY
DAY SO I CAN BE BETTER FOR YOU BOYS!

LOVE, POPS

CONTENTS

006   INTRODUCTION

1 SELF-CARE
SAVAGE UP
011

2 COURAGE
TO HEAL
037

3 FORGIVE
YOURSELF FIRST
063

4 KNOW
YOUR WORTH
089

5 DARE TO FAIL AND
PROTECT YOUR PEACE
115

6 THE ONLY MOMENT
THAT MATTERS
141

7 LEAD BY
EXAMPLE
167

192   THANK YOU
192   ABOUT THE AUTHOR

INTRODUCTION

There was a time in my life when I had given
up on myself. I was exhausted and felt hopeless.
I was raised in a very dysfunctional, mentally
and physically abusive environment fueled
by an alcoholic parent that made me his target
until the age of eight. As an adult, I was still
trying to survive just as I had when I was a child
living in that chaotic environment. Survival
meant not showing my true emotions, never
asking for help, always trying to be perfect and
to please others, in order to keep the illusion
of peace and that everything was okay.
Saying this never worked out for me is
an extreme understatement.

As children, we don't have any developed skills to change our environment, so a lot of us become super skilled at reading and adapting to our environment to feel as safe as possible. There are some survival skills you learn from childhood that can be very handy in life, but most don't transfer well into adult life and will wreak havoc on your relationships and contribute to self-sabotaging behaviors, keeping you from accomplishing goals.

I tried for decades to prove that I was worth something but never could manage to pull it off because the truth was, I had zero self-worth; I was stuck in victim mode, never healing from my past trauma. As every day went by, I hated myself a little bit more, all evidenced by the numerous failures I stacked up with relationships, businesses, and, well, everyday life. But then, by happenstance, I found a trail that led to connecting with nature through hiking and this saved my life. In short, a Self-Care Savage was born!

A "Self-Care Savage" is what I coined to describe myself or anyone who prioritizes their own well-being and takes active steps to maintain their physical, emotional, and mental health. Self-care is becoming increasingly important in today's fast-paced, high-stress world, where people are constantly connected to their devices and bombarded with information and demands. Taking care of yourself is essential for physical, mental, and spiritual well-being.

The term *savage* is used to convey the idea that this person is fiercely committed to their self-care practice and is not afraid to take bold and assertive action to protect their well-being. They prioritize their own needs and make time for self-care, even in the face of competing demands.

In short, a Self-Care Savage is someone who prioritizes their own well-being, takes active steps to maintain their overall health, and is fiercely committed to their self-care practice.

Self-care can take many forms, and what works for one person may not work for another. For me, my Self-Care Savage work began through my connection with nature. Through getting in touch with nature, I connected with myself and believe nature is an antidote for healing. Sometimes changing our surroundings can be such a powerful tool that connects us to who we truly are and helps undo the beliefs that have been ingrained in us since childhood. I use the outdoors as a form of therapy. I believe that connecting to nature and spending time alone is crucial for growth and healing. Being in nature is what heals the mind, body, and soul! It won't heal you for every single thing, and I'm not saying to just go out in nature and everything will be okay, but a little nature will do you some good!

My approach to being a Self-Care Savage involves doing the critical mind-set work to become mentally independent and live outside of others' expectations and impositions. Life is tough, but meeting challenges with discipline, determination, a positive attitude, and mindfulness will most often lead to a meaningful, peaceful, and happy life that will inspire others. Being a Self-Care Savage means being self-reliant and accepting that nobody is coming to save you. We all have trauma from the past and we need to deal with it because we carry it with us every day. You and only you can do the work to heal, forgive yourself first, and clear a path to forgive others. If you are facing challenges in life and are ready to do the Self-Care Savage work of putting yourself first, then you have come to the right place.

In my quest to find healing and in finding nature, I decided to create short videos of myself outdoors giving quick advice or "Friendly

Reminders" and post them online on my social media channel ucanoutdoors. It started out as something to keep myself accountable in doing the work but turned into something much bigger that has helped many people. The reminders in this book are a continuation of my work, and I hope they help you in starting and continuing your own Self-Care Savage work.

In this book, you will find tips for overcoming challenges and being the best that you can be with simple, practical, and useful reminders that you can use every day. You can open the book and read each chapter in order or turn to a random page to read some reminders—there is no perfect way to read this. It's for you, so read it the way that feels best for you! Each chapter is separated by a theme with reminders to help motivate you to let things go, trust in yourself, love yourself, forgive yourself, and find healing. Some reminders have accompanying text to help you delve deeper into the sayings and others stand together on their own pages.

I HOPE THIS BOOK WILL BRAINWASH YOU INTO BELIEVING IN YOURSELF AND FEELING LIKE YOU CAN ACCOMPLISH ANYTHING.

This journey is just the beginning for you—welcome.

CHAPTER 1

SELF-CARE SAVAGE UP

As I explained earlier, a Self-Care Savage is someone who prioritizes their own well-being, takes active steps to maintain their overall health, and is deeply committed to their self-care practice. The Self-Care Savage mentality begins by taking care of yourself first. When you take care of yourself first, whether that is mentally, physically, or otherwise, you will be better prepared to serve others. When you are doing well, you can do well for other people. You can't nourish someone else's cup while yours remains empty—there will be nothing to serve out of.

See how that works? It's not selfish to take care of yourself first—it's selfish not to.

The first step in taking care of yourself and entering the Self-Care Savage mentality is to make a decision right now to take responsibility for everything in your life—the good, the bad, all of it. Taking responsibility is hard work that requires facing all those fears we may have let run freely and unchecked in our minds. These fears usually stem from our childhood environment and the things we learned from them. Some of us may have been exposed to chaos, neglect, physical abuse, mental abuse, or a combination. A lot of us learned to just survive instead of thrive. The things we learned or experienced in our childhoods can become an issue as we move into adulthood.

Our experience as children informs our adult lives. If you came from a chaotic childhood, chances are good that you carry some of those experiences with you and sometimes may even let those experiences drive your decisions. Sure, we may have learned some amazing survival skills that can sometimes serve us well as adults, such as being more cautious around others before trusting them completely. This can be a good thing because then the people in our inner circle are people that we trust completely and we feel have our best interests at heart. But we may also find that these survival skills mostly cause pain, aggravation, and collateral damage with our adult relationships when we have not done the Self-Care Savage work to heal and forgive ourselves. For instance, being overly cautious can keep us from fully trusting others and cause us to get triggered by little things that cause greater issues in our relationships if left unchecked.

Once you have taken responsibility for your adult life, only then can you begin the journey of inner healing and forgiveness. The only way to start to heal and forgive—and when I say forgive, I mean forgiving yourself first, this is very important—is to understand and accept that everything starts with you, with no outside blame or excuses for how you've handled your adult life. When I finally got to this point of taking responsibility, it felt like a dam burst inside of me and so many yucky old feelings broke loose and rushed out of me. I felt lighter, clearer, and more motivated than ever to become a Self-Care Savage!

YOU CANNOT KEEP LIVING IN YOUR PAST.

This does not mean people who do you wrong or have done you wrong should be let off the hook, or that some bad life event that brings disruption is not recognized as such. It means that you take responsibility for how you handle these events and issues without regressing to actions and behaviors that keep you a victim to your past and not moving forward. This means not using your past as an excuse for disruptive behavior. It means not punishing yourself for what happened to you or what other people did to you. It means loving yourself enough to find the space to give yourself kindness, understanding, and compassion. It means giving yourself a better present to thrive and truly live instead of just survive. It means telling yourself that you are enough and worthy of love and everything good. It means looking after yourself and what you need to fill up your cup.

I'm not saying forget your experiences or your past but to accept that there are parts of your adult life within your control.

Accept that the decisions you make affect your current life and that you need to take responsibility for your part in how your adult life is now. By doing that, you will be able to make better decisions for yourself. Maybe you are keeping certain people in your life who suck your energy dry. Ask yourself why and then make the necessary steps to remove those people from your life or create better boundaries in your relationships with these people—this is part of self-care.

Taking accountability for yourself and looking out for your own best interests will take time and a lot of work. But if you are open to taking the first step in being a Self-Care Savage, you will see where you need to focus your attention. You will be able to figure out what parts of your life need healing and some love and then take the necessary steps to show up for yourself when needed. Perhaps you were made to feel as though you were never good enough to warrant kindness, so the work for you now may be showing yourself kindness during difficult moments. Perhaps you need to examine how what you are doing is not benefiting you, and then figure out how you can take responsibility for your life and give yourself what you need to move toward a brighter future.

Life is not easy. You will slip, and you will never be perfect—no one is—but as a Self-Care Savage you will always be the first to take responsibility for yourself and continue to work on healing and forgiving yourself.

The Friendly Reminders in this chapter will help you understand that the importance of self-care first is what makes you better for others. Look through these reminders whenever you need to look out for yourself or when you feel stuck in the same patterns. Whenever you need motivation to do some self-care, these Friendly Reminders will help you move forward in your voyage to a better you.

DO YOU WANT TO

MEET THE LOVE OF YOUR LIFE?

GO LOOK IN THE MIRROR!

You can only love to the level at which you love yourself. You must do the work to fall in love with yourself and be happy with who you are before entering any relationship. Only then can you truly give and receive love in a healthy and fulfilling way.

Others cannot fill the void inside you—only you can do that. Only you can give yourself the most wonderful type of love that you deserve and want. Once you are able to love yourself, then you can love someone else properly as well as they deserve.

Self-love is the foundation of a happy and healthy life. It involves accepting yourself for who you are, flaws and all, and treating yourself with kindness and compassion. This includes taking care of your physical and mental health, setting boundaries, and being true to yourself. When you love yourself, you are more likely to attract people who also love and respect you.

Self-acceptance is also an important aspect of self-love. It means accepting and embracing all parts of yourself, including your past and your present. It's about letting go of the need to be perfect and embracing the reality that everyone is human and makes mistakes. By accepting yourself, you can let go of self-criticism and negative self-talk, which are detrimental to your self-esteem.

Focusing on self-love and self-acceptance is essential for finding happiness in any relationship. It's a journey worth taking, and you deserve it. The love of your life is the one you see in the mirror.

IF YOU NEED
SOMETHING TO BELIEVE IN,
START WITH YOURSELF!

ALWAYS SPEAK HIGHLY
OF YOURSELF.

CELEBRATE YOURSELF; NOBODY
KNOWS WHAT IT TAKES TO BE YOU!

LEARN TO SAY NO, WITHOUT
EXPLAINING YOURSELF.

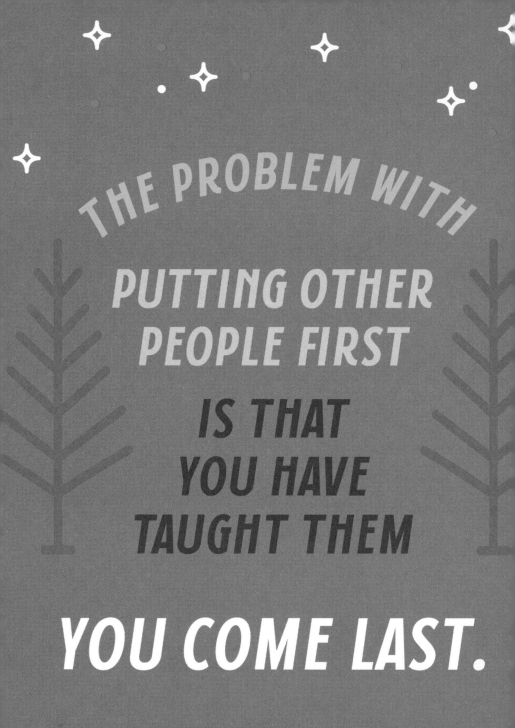

Putting others first can be a positive trait, as it often involves being selfless and considerate of others' needs and wants. However, when taken to an extreme, it can lead to neglecting your own needs and desires. This can create a dynamic in which others come to expect that you will always put them first and may take advantage of this tendency.

When you consistently put others first, you may begin to feel resentful or taken for granted. Additionally, when you don't prioritize your own needs, you may neglect your own well-being and end up feeling burnt out. This can lead to a negative cycle where you feel drained and unable to take care of others or yourself.

Putting others first all the time can also be a form of codependency and a way to avoid dealing with your own issues. It can prevent you from having healthy relationships. Healthy relationships are built on mutual respect and trust, and both parties must have their own needs and wants met.

Work to find a balance between taking care of yourself and others. This means setting boundaries, saying no when necessary, and prioritizing your own needs and wants. It's also important to communicate your needs and desires to others, so they understand that you are not always available to put them first.

It's okay to be there for others sometimes, but remember that you have to be there for yourself too. You are the most important thing on your list. So, put yourself at the top of your own list!

YOU'RE THE CEO OF YOUR OWN LIFE
AND ACCOUNTABLE FOR EVERYTHING
THAT GOES WITH THAT. SO HIRE, FIRE,
AND PROMOTE ACCORDINGLY!

PUT YOURSELF AT THE TOP OF YOUR
OWN LIST, BECAUSE HONESTLY, YOU'RE
NOT AT THE TOP OF ANYBODY ELSE'S.

IT'S TIME TO START LETTING
PEOPLE KNOW IT IS A PRIVILEGE
TO BE IN YOUR LIFE.

IF WHATEVER YOU'RE DOING
RIGHT NOW MAKES YOU HAPPY,
IT DOESN'T HAVE TO MAKE
SENSE TO ANYBODY ELSE.

IT'S YOUR LIFE,

NOT THEIRS.

SELF-CARE SAVAGE WISDOM

Remember that your happiness is your own responsibility, and it is not dependent on the validation or understanding of others. You should do what makes you happy, regardless of whether it makes sense to anyone else.

Too often, people allow themselves to be swayed by the opinions and expectations of others. They may feel pressure to conform to societal norms or live up to the expectations of friends and family. But it is important to remember that you are the only person who truly knows what makes you happy, and you are the only person who can make the decision to pursue that happiness.

It is true that some people may not understand or approve of the choices you make. They may question why you are doing something or criticize your actions. But their opinions do not define you. You are the one who has to live with the choices you make, so make choices that align with your own values and desires.

It is not necessary for you to explain or justify your choices to others. You are not responsible for their understanding or approval.

You do not have to defend yourself or your actions. You have the right to live your life as you see fit, without having to answer to anyone else.

The happiness is yours to live.

YOU'RE ALLOWED TO DO
WHATEVER IS BEST FOR YOU, EVEN IF
IT PISSES EVERYBODY OFF.

○

YOU ARE ALWAYS GOING TO LET
PEOPLE DOWN, JUST MAKE SURE
IT'S NOT YOU ANYMORE.

○

DON'T DENY YOUR FEELINGS AND
EMOTIONS JUST TO MAKE EVERYONE
ELSE COMFORTABLE.

○

STOP SETTING YOURSELF ON
FIRE TO KEEP OTHERS WARM!

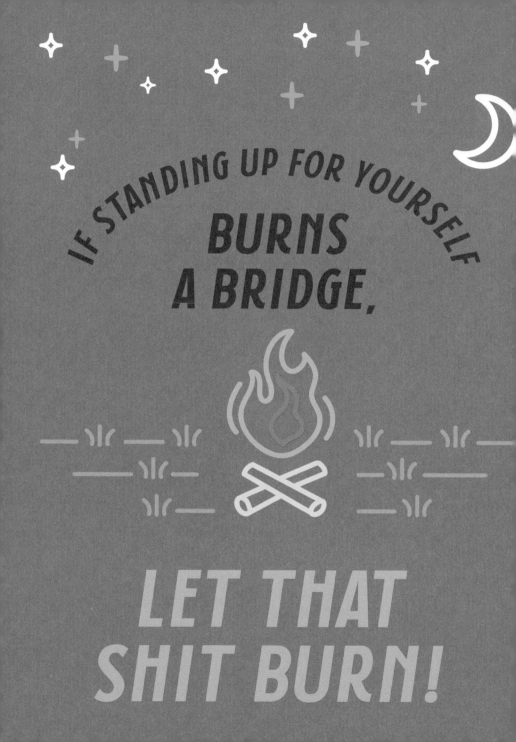

You have to be okay with standing up for yourself, even if that means losing people. Sometimes you have to love yourself enough to let go of people who are not doing you any good.

However, before you do burn a bridge, it is also important to weigh the importance of the relationship versus the issue at hand. In some cases, it may be worth sacrificing the relationship in order to stand up for what you believe in. For example, if the relationship is toxic or if the other person is treating you poorly, it may be best to walk away.

On the other hand, if the relationship is important to you and the issue at hand is not a significant one, it may be better to find a compromise or another way to address the issue without burning the bridge. Additionally, if the other person is willing to work through the issue and find a resolution, it may be worth trying to save the relationship.

Ultimately, the decision of whether or not to burn a bridge is a personal one and depends on the specific circumstances of the situation. Always try to communicate clearly and effectively to find a mutually beneficial solution. If that can't be done, then light the match, let it burn, and move on!

Don't be afraid to let go of people. You come first, and you are your own hero.

IN THE PROCESS OF LOSING
SOMEONE YOU FIND YOURSELF;
THAT'S NOT A LOSS—THAT'S A WIN!

○

PEOPLE MAY NOT ALWAYS TELL YOU
HOW THEY FEEL ABOUT YOU, BUT
THEY WILL ALWAYS SHOW YOU.

○

STOP BEING THE GO-TO PERSON
FOR SOMEONE YOU CAN'T GO TO!

LEARN TO BE OKAY

WITH PEOPLE NOT KNOWING YOUR SIDE OF THE STORY.

YOU DON'T HAVE TO PROVE ANYTHING TO ANYBODY.

It can be difficult to accept that not everyone will understand your perspective or agree with you. It's not their responsibility to do so, just as it is not your responsibility to convince them to see things your way. Instead, focus on understanding and respecting their point of view.

You cannot control what others think or say about you. You can only control your own actions and reactions.

By letting go of the need to prove yourself to others, you free yourself from the stress and anxiety that come with trying to constantly justify your actions.

It's important to be comfortable with standing alone in your beliefs. At times, you may be the only person who holds a certain opinion. It's okay to be different, and it's okay to have a different perspective.

The most important thing is to live your life in a way that is authentic and true to your values. Only then can you build deeper and more meaningful relationships with others.

The only person who has to be okay with your side of the story is YOU.

YOU ARE THE MOST **PERMANENT PERSON IN YOUR LIFE,** *SO ALWAYS CHOOSE YOU!*

Choosing yourself means putting your own needs and wants first and making choices that align with your values and goals. When you choose yourself, you take responsibility for your own happiness and well-being. This means setting boundaries, saying no to things that don't serve you, even if it disappoints others, and making time for self-care and self-improvement. It also means being honest with yourself about your strengths and weaknesses, and working to improve in areas where you may be lacking.

One of the most important aspects of choosing yourself is setting boundaries with people. This means knowing your limits and communicating them clearly to others. Setting boundaries can be difficult, but it is necessary for maintaining a healthy and fulfilling life.

Another important aspect of choosing yourself is self-care. This means taking care of your physical, emotional, and mental well-being. It can include things like eating well, getting enough sleep, exercising, and practicing mindfulness or meditation. It's also important to make time for hobbies or activities that bring you joy, as well as for rest and relaxation.

Self-improvement is key when choosing yourself. This means being open to learning and growing, being willing to take risks and stepping out of your comfort zone. It may not always be easy, but it's a rewarding journey that will lead you to a joyous life.

CHAPTER 2

COURAGE TO HEAL

Some of you may be thinking, "Oh no, I don't want to feel! It hurts so bad!" But healing takes courage. If you don't feel the hurts of the past so you can heal, you'll stay a victim and spew it all over your relationships and the world around you. That is what victims do!

There's immediate comfort with deflecting, then blaming and excusing your inappropriate behaviors so you don't have to feel the pain and hurts from the past. Of course, this is only temporary and will always end up rearing its ugly head in other ways again and again. How's that been working for you?

Never worked for me, either!

When you have a victim mentality, you stay stuck in your pain without a way out. You keep repeating the same patterns and making the same destructive decisions that lead to you living a life you aren't happy in. As I explained in the previous chapter, I'm not saying that you don't hold people accountable for their actions or that you don't acknowledge your experiences. I'm saying that you don't want to stay stuck in destructive behavior so that you aren't able to move toward a place of healing.

When you move away from being the victim, you can take action toward healing and create positive changes in your life. The only way to create change in your life is to acknowledge where you are and to acknowledge your pain so that you can face it head on and start to work on what needs to be healed. Healing leads to clearer decisions for yourself and for your relationships, a sharper mind, and a lighter you.

Sometimes we may not realize how deep our trauma goes and how much of our childhood pain affects our current reality. But when we choose to feel what has caused us pain rather than run away from it, we choose to change for the better. It takes a lot of strength and bravery to create change in your life because it means facing your biggest fears. Perhaps your first heartbreak came from one or both of your parents and that pain makes you fearful of finding love now and so you push people away to keep from getting hurt. Pain is fear, and our fears keep us from living our best lives. Facing our pain means facing our fears. That's part of what courage is about: facing our fears even when we are scared.

Maybe the example above doesn't have anything to do with you, or maybe it does. The point is that you have to look within to find what needs to be tended to and then do the inner work to heal so that you are moving closer to the life you want and deserve.

Be real with yourself and what is keeping you from living in your happiness and then do the work to start to heal what you need to. Ask yourself the hard questions. When you are being triggered by something, even if it feels like something small, ask yourself why. Are you really mad at your partner for leaving socks on the floor or is there something deeper going on? Perhaps you feel as if your partner does not listen to you, and it makes you feel alone, just like you were made to feel as a child. Again, this may not be you, but it's an example of how small triggers can mean there might be something bigger going on, that there is pain you may have to acknowledge. Make the brave choice to heal yourself so that you can continue to nourish your soul.

Healing will take time, and you may find yourself going back to your old patterns again because that is the way of life. You will not be changed in a day or even in a few months. You can't undo years of learning in a short period of time. Remember to show yourself grace whenever you find yourself making the same decisions that don't benefit you. Healing is constant. You have to constantly be working on healing yourself.

Healing looks different for everyone, and there are different ways of healing yourself. For one person, healing can include seeing a medical professional. For someone else, healing can be taking care of their own needs. For me, it is nature. For others, it can be a combination of many things. The key is to find out what has to be healed so you can take the necessary steps to get what you need.

DON'T BE AFRAID TO FACE YOUR FEARS.

Don't be afraid to face what has been hurting you. You are in power now. Step into your courage and set yourself free from your pain. You are the only one who can make the decision for you. Yes, it's scary to create change in your life, to face things head on that have been hurting you for years, but in the end, you create the change you want in your life. Sure, there are things outside of our control. Life happens unexpectedly and some storms will take us by surprise and require a long time to get through, but know that there is always a light at the end of it all.

We can't control what happens around us all the time, but we can control what we do with the hand we are dealt. You are more powerful than you think. And while there are things that feel like they might break us, they only make us stronger . . . and braver.

Fight through the fear and pain by giving yourself the courage to heal.

The Friendly Reminders in this chapter will light that healing fire inside you and help you remember how strong and courageous you are.

IT'S OKAY
TO NOT BE OKAY,

IT'S JUST NOT OKAY
TO STAY THAT WAY.

SELF-CARE SAVAGE WISDOM

It is normal to experience difficult emotions and mental health challenges. Everyone goes through difficult times, and it is important to take care of yourself during these periods, to take action to address these challenges, and to work toward improving your health. This can involve seeking help from a therapist or counselor, talking to friends and family, practicing self-care, and making lifestyle changes to promote your overall well-being.

Reaching out and asking for help when you need it is a sign of strength, not weakness. Talk to a therapist or counselor, join a support group, or speak with a trusted friend or family member. These individuals can provide you with support, guidance, and practical advice.

Self-care is also an important aspect of mental health. This includes taking care of your physical well-being through exercise, healthy eating, getting enough sleep, and addressing any underlying physical health conditions; engaging in activities that bring you joy; spending time with loved ones; practicing mindfulness, such as meditation, yoga, and journaling; and reducing stress through time-management techniques, setting realistic goals, and learning to say no to unnecessary commitments.

Be patient with yourself. Setbacks are a normal part of the process. Healing and forgiveness are always doable when you Self-Care Savage Up. When you incorporate the right support and make the effort, you can be unstoppable in improving your life.

YOU'RE ALWAYS ONE DECISION AWAY
FROM A TOTALLY DIFFERENT LIFE!

○

YOU CAN'T WAIT UNTIL LIFE ISN'T
HARD ANYMORE BEFORE YOU
DECIDE TO BE HAPPY.

○

STOP CHOOSING WHAT ISN'T
CHOOSING YOU!

○

HAPPINESS IS AN INSIDE JOB.

STOP TELLING YOURSELF

IT WILL GET BETTER.

IT NEVER WILL!

START TELLING YOURSELF

YOU HAVE TO GET BETTER.

It is more productive to focus on actively working toward improvement than waiting passively for it to happen. Once you figure out what needs to get better, then you can start to shift your mind-set by breaking down your larger goals into smaller, specific, more manageable steps that you can focus on. You can't make big changes in a day, but small steps, small changes, lead to progress, and thus big changes. Smaller goals also help you see tangible progress and stay motivated. The point is that only you can make the changes you want to see in your life. Start with a small step and see where that takes you.

Another helpful strategy is to surround yourself with positive and supportive people. Whether it's friends, family, or a therapist, having a support system can be a valuable resource for encouragement, advice, and accountability.

Self-Care Savage Up and start growing your self-worth. Remember, change and progress take time, but with hard work and determination, you can make meaningful improvements in your life. Seek professional help if you need it.

It is important to have a positive attitude when facing challenges or difficult situations. When things don't go as planned, be kind to yourself. Celebrate your achievements no matter how small. Any little step is a step closer to change.

Focus on actively working toward improvement. Get better, be better!

PEOPLE ARE GOING TO COME
AND GO IN YOUR LIFE, BUT THAT
PERSON IN THE MIRROR IS GOING
TO BE THERE FOREVER, SO TAKE
CARE OF YOURSELF!

WHEN SOMEONE STEPS OVER
ONE OF YOUR BOUNDARIES,
STOP MOVING THE BOUNDARY AND
START MOVING THE PERSON.

LOSE AS MANY PEOPLE AS
YOU NEED TO IN ORDER
NOT TO LOSE YOURSELF.

STOP
DISAPPOINTING
YOURSELF

BY EXPECTING BETTER
FROM OTHERS.

SELF-CARE SAVAGE WISDOM

Everyone has their own strengths, weaknesses, and limitations, and it's important to respect them and work with them, not against them. Expecting better from others can and most often will lead to disappointment and frustration. People will not always meet our expectations, just like we won't always meet others' expectations.

One way to avoid disappointment is to set realistic expectations of others. Understand that everyone makes mistakes and has their own unique challenges. We are all imperfect. By setting realistic expectations, you are more likely to be satisfied with their actions and less likely to be disappointed.

Also, instead of focusing on what others are not doing or should be doing, focus on what you're doing and can do to improve yourself and your own situation. Communicate clearly with others about your needs and expectations so they understand what you are asking of them. This can help prevent misunderstandings and ensure that everyone is on the same page.

Instead of trying to change or control others, focus on what you can do to improve yourself. When you commit to becoming a Self-Care Savage, you will focus on your own growth and development, and you will stop being disappointed by others. Work on being a better version of you. There is plenty of work to do right here.

THERE'S REALLY NO REASON TO CUT
PEOPLE OFF—JUST KEEP HEALING AND
GROWING AND THEY'LL FALL OFF.

NO MATTER HOW MUCH YOU
LOVE THEM, SOME PEOPLE ARE
JUST NOT GOOD FOR YOU.

YOU HAVE TO MEET PEOPLE
WHERE THEY ARE AND SOMETIMES
YOU HAVE TO LEAVE THEM THERE.

YOUR TASTE IN PEOPLE WILL CHANGE
AS YOU START LOVING YOURSELF.

LIFE DOESN'T HAVE A REMOTE:

YOU'RE GOING TO HAVE TO GET OFF YOUR BUTT AND CHANGE IT YOURSELF!

Life is not something that can be controlled or manipulated from a distance, but rather requires active participation and effort. Self-Care Savage Up and start making positive changes in your life by taking personal responsibility, setting clear goals, developing a plan of action, and consistently working toward achieving them.

Setting clear and achievable goals may involve identifying specific areas of your life that you would like to improve, such as relationships, career, or personal health and wellness. Once these goals have been identified, develop a plan of action that includes specific steps and milestones that will help you achieve them.

When making changes in your life, it's important to take consistent and persistent action. This can involve making small but meaningful changes on a regular basis, such as incorporating healthy habits into your daily routine, or taking steps to improve your skills and qualifications in a specific area.

Be resilient and adapt to the changes that come along with the journey of achieving goals, and don't give up when things don't go as planned. Be open to new opportunities, learn from your failures, and try to be more optimistic. Self-Care Savage work is a continuous process of self-improvement and requires a lot of hard work and dedication, but the rewards are worth it.

IF YOU'RE NOT WILLING TO FIGHT
FOR YOURSELF TO GET BETTER, THEN
STOP WHINING WHEN YOU DON'T.

○

YOU CAN'T CHANGE PEOPLE AROUND
YOU, BUT YOU CAN CHANGE THE
PEOPLE AROUND YOU.

○

THERE'S NO ELEVATOR IN HEALING;
YOU'VE GOT TO TAKE THE STAIRS
AND DO THE WORK!

TIME DOESN'T HEAL.

IT'S WHAT YOU DO WITH THE TIME.

Simply waiting for time to pass will not necessarily bring about healing. Just like a physical injury requires engaging in rehabilitation to heal appropriately, you have to actively work through emotions, past traumas, and repairing relationships to heal.

It is essential to process the emotions associated with a traumatic event or difficult situation. This can be done through therapy, journaling, talking with friends and family, or engaging in activities that bring a sense of peace and calm. Avoiding or suppressing emotions can lead to longer-term issues such as depression and anxiety.

When it comes to relationships, time alone will not repair a broken bond. It requires effort and communication from both parties to understand and work through issues. A willingness to forgive, to compromise, and to actively listen are all important for repairing a relationship More often than not, healing will have to be done from a distance because the wounds cut too deep to have any type of communication. Other times, you may want or need to seek a professional to help in repairing relationships.

The saying "time heals all wounds" is not entirely true. It is what you do with the time that counts. Some pain may feel duller over time but will not ever completely go away, even when you work through it. But when you put in the work to heal, in time, you will feel lighter. You will start to see and feel peace in your life.

WHEN YOU'VE HEALED A PIECE OF YOU,

YOU'LL START TELLING THAT STORY DIFFERENTLY.

SELF-CARE SAVAGE WISDOM

Healing is necessary so you can flip the narrative on your past hurts and trauma from one of negative emotions to one of acceptance and learning. When we heal from an emotional injury, we often reflect on the experience and how it has changed us. As we come to terms with what we have been through, our perspective shifts and we begin to see things in a new light.

For example, if someone has gone through childhood abuse like I did, they may be feeling scared and defeated. But as they begin to do the Self-Care Savage work to heal from those traumas and forgive themselves and those involved, their outlook changes. They start to see those past traumas as a test of their resilience, and they continue to learn from it as needed.

Similarly, if someone has gone through a difficult emotional experience, such as a breakup or the loss of a loved one, they may initially feel overwhelmed with grief. But as they begin to process their emotions and find ways to cope, their perspective may shift. They may start to see the experience as an opportunity for growth and begin to appreciate the lessons they have learned.

In both cases, the individual's story may become one of resilience, perseverance, and hope, rather than one of defeat and despair.

It's okay to feel a range of emotions and it's okay to take the time you need to heal. Do the work to Self-Care Savage Up, and now when you tell your story, it will help others!

CHAPTER 3

FORGIVE YOURSELF FIRST

Do you ever struggle forgiving others
when they do you wrong? Sometimes
when someone does you wrong you may
want revenge. You want them to be held
accountable and pay for treating you poorly,
especially if you feel it was intentional.
Usually when someone does something
to hurt us, the first thing we do is feel angry
and hurt, and sometimes what we want
to do is get back at them. And, yes,
we have a right to be angry
and hurt and all of that is normal.

But, oftentimes, we get caught up in revenge, in holding on to a lot of anger and then let this anger drive us. The thing is that this feeling of revenge, of pain, of anger lingers in everything that we do. When we keep ourselves in pain, we are not able to see anything past that. We allow the other person to have control over our lives and drive our decisions because when we hold on to this feeling of revenge, that's what we keep thinking about. We focus on the other person and what they did wrong instead of focusing on ourselves and what we need. I was very skilled at giving all those that did me wrong all my power, which kept me in a victim mentality. Victim mentality is a bad place to be and brought me zero positive results.

This thought of revenge makes it easier for you to focus on the other person's poor behavior and keeps you from looking at your own behavior, firing up the blame game. This doesn't mean you can't or shouldn't hold the other person accountable for their actions. They should be held accountable, but there are times when we need to also look at what we are allowing to enter into our lives. Sometimes, we have to look at our own behaviors and what we believe we deserve. If you don't think you are deserving of love, then you will keep allowing people who are not loving into your life.

And when someone does hurt us, we want to hold on to this hurt so badly that we forget how much damage we are doing to ourselves by holding on to pain. We may not have control over everything in our lives, but we do have control over how we react to something and how we use our reactions to move forward in life.

Don't let someone else's hurtful behavior dictate your life and how you react to things. The longer you hold on to things, the less you are able to let go of them and the more you focus on the wrong things.

The only thing holding on to grudges really accomplishes is you staying angry and resentful. This is very disrespectful to yourself because you aren't solving what is happening within you that makes you think you deserve people like this in your life or deserve anger taking over your thoughts. This thought process will keep you from healing because you will be focusing on someone else's behavior instead of your own.

Forgiving others never starts with them, it always starts with you! To give that true real forgiveness to others, you will have to go through yourself first. Self-Care Savage Up and start forgiving yourself for your imperfections, all the inappropriate things you did, and all the things you didn't do.

You have to forgive yourself for whatever behaviors or patterns are hurting you. Forgive yourself for not always having the answers, for perhaps not putting up necessary boundaries, for not being perfect all the time. Forgive yourself for your past. You can't go back, you can only move forward. Forgive yourself so that you can forgive others and let things go that don't serve you. You don't deserve to be in pain. You deserve to move forward in healing and in happiness.

Think (and journal) about what you need to forgive yourself for and how that might be affecting your decisions today. What are some things you can start forgiving yourself for? What are some things that might take you a while to forgive yourself for but you are aware of now? How can you give yourself more compassion? How can you move toward a place of forgiveness?

BE KINDER TO YOURSELF.
YOU DESERVE IT.

If you don't believe that you deserve forgiveness, you won't be able to give yourself the life you deserve. You won't believe that you are worthy of a good life, which you are. You are worthy of living a healed life.

When you understand you're not perfect and you will make lots of mistakes in life, then you can accept them and start taking responsibility for them. Once you do that, you can give yourself compassion, and then you can start to understand that nobody else is perfect and be able to have compassion for them.

Compassion for yourself leads you to forgive yourself, which then leads to forgiving others and the big payoff: peace! When it comes to forgiving others, it is not for them, it is for you. Holding on to pain doesn't serve you at all. When you learn to let things go, you are able to move toward a place of tranquility.

Forgiveness is never easy, and it can take a long time to get to a place where you can finally forgive yourself and others. Don't beat yourself up for not getting there as quickly as you want to or are prepared for. As I keep saying, nobody is perfect, and you can't just turn on a switch and everything is okay. Take it day by day. And remember, the key to forgiving others starts with forgiving yourself first.

The Friendly Reminders in this chapter will help you internalize the many benefits of self-forgiveness. Remind yourself that you are worthy of forgiveness, of a life full of peace and love. It all starts with you.

REAL GROWTH

ONLY HAPPENS WHEN
YOU GET TIRED OF
YOUR OWN SHIT!

SELF-CARE SAVAGE WISDOM

Real growth happens when a person is willing to confront and overcome their own shortcomings and take the necessary steps to improve themselves. This means being honest with yourself about your flaws and taking the necessary steps to address them, rather than ignoring or denying them. Acknowledging your flaws and doing the work to address them can be difficult and uncomfortable, but it is necessary for real change to occur. It can be helpful to surround yourself with people who will support and encourage this process of growth, rather than enabling negative patterns or habits.

Sometimes we allow ourselves to live in misery because it's comfortable for us. When we are used to being in pain and it's all we know, we tend to make choices that lead back to pain, whether that's continuing negative behaviors or continuing to allow people to enter our lives knowing they may not be good for us. Only when you get tired of your own shit will you be able to make positive changes in your life.

Personal growth can happen in a variety of ways and can also involve learning new skills, taking on new challenges, and being open to new experiences. Personal growth is a continuous journey that requires self-awareness, commitment, and persistence. Be prepared to face setbacks and challenges along the way, and not be discouraged by them. It is not an easy journey, but you will love yourself more for it in the end.

HOLDING YOURSELF ACCOUNTABLE
IS DIFFERENT THAN BEATING
YOURSELF UP.

NO MATTER HOW FAR YOU'VE
GONE ON THE WRONG PATH,
YOU CAN STILL TURN AROUND.

IT'S TIME NOW TO FORGIVE
YOURSELF FOR ALL THE
THINGS YOU DIDN'T DO.

HONESTY SAVES EVERYONE'S TIME!

YES,
THEY DID YOU WRONG,

**BUT YOU DO
YOURSELF WRONG**

THE LONGER YOU
HOLD ON TO IT.

Holding on to anger or resentment toward someone who has wronged you can be harmful to your own well-being. It can lead to stress and depression and negatively impact your relationships. It's important to recognize that forgiving others is not about excusing their behavior, but rather about releasing the hold that it has on you.

One way to start the process of forgiveness is to practice empathy. Try to understand the other person's perspective and consider the reasons why they may have acted the way they did. This can help reduce feelings of anger and resentment.

Another technique is to focus on the present moment. Instead of dwelling on past events, try to be mindful of the present and focus on what you can do in the moment to improve your situation. And finally, practice gratitude. Reflect on the things in your life that you are thankful for and remember that forgiveness is a gift you give to yourself. It allows you to let go of the past and move forward in a positive direction.

Forgiveness is a process. It's okay if it takes time to forgive someone, and it may not happen overnight. Enlisting professional help or talking to a friend, family member, or counselor can help you process the feelings and emotions that come with forgiveness.

Stop disrespecting yourself by holding on to things that are not doing you any good.

INSTEAD OF FOCUSING ON
SOMEONE ELSE'S TOXIC BEHAVIOR,
MAYBE YOU SHOULD FOCUS ON
YOUR OWN FOR A MINUTE.

WHEN YOU GIVE SOMEONE THE
POWER TO BE THE SOURCE OF YOUR
HAPPINESS, YOU ALSO GIVE THEM THE
POWER TO MAKE YOU MISERABLE.

YOU HAVE NO NEED FOR REVENGE,
YOU'RE NO LONGER IN THEIR LIFE,
AND THAT'S PUNISHMENT ENOUGH!

SOMETIMES YOU HAVE TO

FORGET HOW YOU FEEL AND

REMEMBER WHAT YOU DESERVE!

Emotions can cloud our judgment and make it difficult to remember what we truly deserve. When we are feeling down or mistreated, it can be easy to accept less than what we deserve in our relationships, at work, or in any other aspect of our lives.

This is especially true when we are in relationships with people who don't know how to love us properly. When you don't know how to love yourself properly, you forget that you are worth the world, and you allow someone to make you feel less than. When you don't value yourself because you haven't forgiven yourself for your past actions, you let other people tell you what you are worth. Sometimes when we love someone and they hurt us, our feelings for them or what we allow them to do to us make us forget what we deserve.

Part of putting yourself first means forgiving yourself so that you don't let emotions cloud your judgment and can make positive decisions. It is okay to leave a situation or a person that is not treating you well or making you unhappy. You deserve to be in a place where you are valued and respected.

One way to remind ourselves of what we deserve is to make a list of our own personal values and what we believe is important in our lives. This can include things like honesty, loyalty, respect, and kindness. By keeping this list in mind, we can remind ourselves that these are the things we should be expecting and accepting in our relationships and interactions with others.

Only you get to decide what you deserve. Make choices that are worthy of you.

THE WORLD WILL KNOCK YOU
DOWN ENOUGH, YOU DON'T NEED
TO DO IT YOURSELF.

○

ANYTHING THAT COSTS YOU YOUR
MENTAL HEALTH IS TOO EXPENSIVE.

○

JUST BECAUSE THINGS COULD HAVE
BEEN DIFFERENT DOESN'T MEAN
THEY WOULD HAVE BEEN BETTER.

○

SOMETIMES THE DISRESPECT IS
ALL THE CLOSURE YOU NEED.

STOP FIGHTING YOUR WAY INTO OTHER PEOPLE'S HEARTS, AND FIGHT YOUR WAY INTO YOUR OWN HEART!

Self-worth, self-love, and self-acceptance are important steps in becoming a well-rounded and fulfilled individual. Instead of focusing on winning over others and looking for approval and love, try to focus on understanding yourself, accepting yourself, and, of course, loving yourself. Take the time to explore your thoughts, feelings, and beliefs. Reflect on your past experiences and work on healing the trauma and hurts so you can forgive yourself and have a clear path to forgive others.

Stop focusing on how you can be better for others and how you can get others to love you. Focus on how you can strengthen the love you have for yourself. How can you show yourself more love today? Stop focusing on what you need to forgive others for and focus on what you need to forgive yourself for. What is it that you haven't forgiven yourself for that keeps you from showing yourself love?

Think about how you can use your strengths to improve yourself and your life. Identify areas of your life that you want to improve and create a plan to achieve what you want. This can be anything from learning a new skill to developing a more positive attitude. Spend time in nature to help you get a clearer understanding of yourself.

Foster self-love and fight your way into your own heart so that you have something to give when others let you into theirs. Discover your true self. Be patient and persistent. And don't let up.

THERE ARE SOME PEOPLE
YOU JUST HAVE TO LOVE
FROM A DISTANCE.

○

YOU'VE GOT ENOUGH PROBLEMS
OF YOUR OWN FOR ONE PERSON,
SO STOP TRYING TO PACK IN
EVERYONE ELSE'S.

○

STOP ARGUING WITH PEOPLE;
IT'S A TIME WASTER.
JUST LET THEM BE WRONG!

YOUR RELATIONSHIP WITH YOURSELF SETS THE TONE

FOR ALL THE OTHER RELATIONSHIPS THAT YOU HAVE.

SELF-CARE SAVAGE WISDOM

Having a positive and healthy relationship with yourself is essential for your overall self-worth and happiness. When you are comfortable and confident in who you are, you are better able to navigate the relationships and interactions with others. Conversely, when you struggle with self-doubt, insecurity, or self-esteem issues, it can negatively impact your relationships with others.

One key aspect of fostering a healthy relationship with yourself is self-awareness. This includes understanding your own thoughts, feelings, and behaviors, as well as recognizing your strengths and limitations. When you Self-Care Savage Up, you have a clear understanding of yourself and you're better able to communicate your needs and boundaries to others, leading to more fulfilling and satisfying relationships. Once you are self-aware, you are able to forgive yourself and can move toward a healthier relationship with yourself.

Having a positive relationship with yourself also involves positive self-talk. When you feel a negative thought taking over, try to turn it into something positive. Turn a "I can't do this!" into a "I'm still learning, and I can do this!"

Having high self-worth sets the tone for all of your other relationships and interactions, and helps you navigate the world with confidence and ease. When you take the time to understand and care for yourself, and talk to yourself positively, you are better able to connect with others in meaningful and fulfilling ways.

ONCE YOU REALIZE
YOU CAN DO
IT ALONE,

YOU BECOME A
VERY POWERFUL PERSON.

Realizing that you can do things on your own can be empowering and give you a sense of self-worth and self-sufficiency. It can help you become more confident in your abilities and trust your decision-making. When you know that you can rely on yourself, you may be more likely to take on new challenges and opportunities.

Being independent does not mean that you have to do everything alone; it means that you have the ability to take care of yourself and make things happen without relying on others. You can still seek help, advice, and support from others, but you are not dependent on them to achieve your goals.

When you can do things on your own, it can also help you form stronger relationships with others. When you are not overly reliant on others, they are more likely to see you as an equal and be willing to work with you.

Doing things alone and being independent also means being able to take responsibility for your own actions and the outcomes of those actions. It means being accountable for your own successes and failures and learning from both. Taking accountability permits you to see where you may need some forgiveness and then take the necessary steps in forgiving yourself so that you can grow and develop as a person.

Being independent makes you more resilient in the face of adversity. It helps you see how powerful you really are and that you are capable of change and growth. It makes you a badass!

CHAPTER 4

KNOW YOUR WORTH

How much are you worth? Do you know your worth? And when I talk about worth, I'm not talking about money or success. I'm talking about how much love, peace, and happiness you think you are worth.

Most of us cannot answer these very crucial questions. I couldn't answer them until I was in my early fifties. Yep, I spent decades living and feeling as if I wasn't worthy of sustained peace, love, or happiness. And, if I did start getting a glimpse of some peace, love, or happiness, I literally couldn't take it, so I would do what any person with no self-worth would do: I would self-sabotage it all.

Self-worth is the sense of your own value as a person. Most of our self-esteem is driven by external circumstances. We often base our self-worth on some societal standard of worthiness or "enough" we can never achieve. Do I have enough success? Do I make enough money? Am I beautiful enough? Am I smart enough? Am I worthy? The questions never stop, and we never seem to feel like we are worthy or enough. There's always something we have to work on, some unmeasurable standard that we can't keep up with.

When you let your self-worth be determined by external things, you give up control over your own life. This means you make your everyday decisions based on what others will think instead of what you think, always worried about failing. You end up living life in a defensive mind-set, all because you have low or no self-worth. It can be exhausting.

We typically use social media as a way to measure our worthiness. We compare our lives to someone else's photos to feed into our insecurities. I'm here to tell you that not everything is what it seems. Someone's photo or video does not tell the whole truth, and even if it did, your self-worth should not be measured by what you do or don't have.

YOU ARE WORTHY OF EVERYTHING GOOD.

You have to believe it before you start living by this. If you don't believe that you are worthy of good things, then you will not allow good things to happen to you. You can't live life running someone else's race. You are on your own path and sometimes that path can be rocky or longer than those of others, but it is yours and it is still a great path. Everybody is different and therefore everyone's path will be different. Some people will have it harder than others, but that doesn't mean they are any less worthy.

No one will believe that you are worthy of love, happiness, or peace unless you believe it. You can't expect others to believe in you if you don't believe in yourself. You won't get that job if you don't think you're good enough to get it. You won't get those amazing opportunities if you don't believe you should get the chance to partake in them. Having confidence in yourself is everything. When you believe you deserve the very best the world can offer, you start to live your life based on your standards. You start to smile more. You start to see the possibilities in the unknown.

When we don't believe we are deserving of things, we get comfortable with self-sabotage. We start to think that we only deserve the bad stuff that happens to us. That inner voice is our biggest and worst critic. We are our own worst enemies. Whenever we feel that something good is happening in our lives, that's when our inner critic comes into play, to tell us we are not worth it. Our negative thoughts about ourselves can lead us to act in destructive, self-sabotaging ways because we are accustomed to invalidating our self-worth.

One way to combat your inner critic is to tackle it straight on. Whenever you feel a negative thought start to creep in, acknowledge it, and then stop it in its tracks and think something good about yourself. For example, if you are thinking, "I don't believe I'm worthy of this," reframe the thought to "I am ever evolving, and I'm worthy of all the good things."

Self-worth is not about what you can do or what you can achieve or the amount of money you make, but about what makes you, well, you. Self-worth is about who you are as a person to the core of you. Who are you? And, I'll ask that question again: How much do you think you are worth? And this time, say it with me: "I'm worthy of it all—the love, the peace, the happiness." Look at yourself in the mirror and say this to yourself as many times as you can. Say it before you go to bed. Say it when you wake up in the morning. Write it on a sticky note and post it where you will see it every day.

There will be times when you feel the need to compare yourself because that is what people have been conditioned to do. But whenever you feel yourself comparing your life to someone else's or your inner critic begins to take over your thoughts, show yourself some grace. Remind yourself that you are worth more than these external things and only you get to determine your self-worth. And you are worth everything great and then some.

You have the ability to Self-Care Savage Up and do the work to flip this low or no self-worth mind-set into a high self-worth mind-set.

The Friendly Reminders in this chapter will help you focus on yourself. They will help remind you of your worth and that you are in control of your destiny.

WHEN YOU START

SEEING YOUR OWN SELF-WORTH,

THEN YOU'LL STOP WASTING YOUR TIME AROUND PEOPLE WHO DON'T.

When you have a strong sense of self-worth, you are less likely to waste time around people who do not value or respect you. You will start seeking out and surrounding yourself with individuals who treat you well and value your presence.

It also means being able to set healthy boundaries and say no to people or situations that do not align with your values or goals. It means valuing and prioritizing your own needs and wants, and not constantly sacrificing them for those of others.

Developing a strong sense of self-worth can be a lifelong process that requires addressing past traumas, negative beliefs, and patterns of behavior that have contributed to a lack of self-worth.

When you have negative thoughts about yourself it can be hard to see our own value. By overwhelming those negative thoughts with positive thoughts,

you will start to see yourself in a more positive light.

The best way to build and maintain a strong self-worth is by developing a Self-Care Savage routine. This means taking care of your mind, body, and soul by being in nature, exercising, reading, journaling, and doing things that make you happy.

Ultimately, building self-worth is about learning to love and accept yourself, flaws and all. It's about recognizing our own value and strengths, and not relying on external validation or acceptance from others. Your time is important, so value it and care about yourself enough to use it wisely.

YOU DON'T FIND YOUR WORTH IN ANOTHER
PERSON; YOU FIND YOUR WORTH WITHIN
YOURSELF AND THEN YOU FIND PEOPLE
WHO ARE WORTHY OF YOU.

STOP LETTING PEOPLE SAVE YOU
FOR LATER—KNOW YOUR WORTH!

YOUR WORTH IS NOT UP FOR DEBATE;
TAKE MIXED SIGNALS AS A NO.

YOU'RE JUST AS IMPORTANT AS
EVERYBODY ELSE, SO ACT LIKE IT!

IT DOESN'T MATTER IF
**YOU CAN'T DO IT
LIKE THEM**

BECAUSE

**THEY CAN'T DO
IT LIKE YOU!**

SELF-CARE SAVAGE WISDOM

Everyone is different and has their own traits. Just because someone else may be better at something doesn't mean that you are not capable in your own way. It is easy to compare ourselves to others and feel inadequate, but it is vital to focus on what we have to offer.

No one can ever do something exactly like you. We all have our own unique perspectives, experiences, and talents that make us special. Instead of focusing on what others can do that you can't, focus on what you can do that others can't. Embrace your unique skills and talents and use them to your advantage.

Just because someone may seem to have it all together doesn't mean that they don't have their own struggles and difficulties. Be kind and understanding toward others, because you never know what someone else may be going through.

Everyone has their own path in life and it's not a competition with you. You don't have to be better than anyone else to be successful or happy. You just need to be the best version of yourself that you can be. Self-Care Savage Up and work on yourself to be a little better than yesterday.

Celebrate your own talents and use them to make a difference in the world. Remember that you are valuable and capable in your own way, and that's what makes you special. Do it your way, because it's the best way for you!

PEOPLE ARE GOING TO CRITICIZE
YOU NO MATTER WHAT YOU
DO, SO YOU MIGHT AS WELL DO
WHATEVER YOU WANT TO.

○

WHO YOU ARE WHEN NO ONE
IS LOOKING IS WHO YOU ARE.

○

BE YOURSELF, THERE'S NO ONE
BETTER AT IT THAN YOU.

STOP WONDERING
IF YOU'RE GOOD ENOUGH
FOR OTHER PEOPLE,
AND START WONDERING
WHETHER THOSE PEOPLE ARE
GOOD ENOUGH FOR YOU!

SELF-CARE SAVAGE WISDOM

It's not productive to compare yourself to others and wonder whether you're good enough for them. Instead, concentrate on what you bring to a relationship or situation. Surround yourself with people who value you for who you are.

Self-Care Savage Up and shift your perspective. Start wondering whether the people in your life are good enough for you instead of wondering whether you are good enough for them. Take the time to reflect on what you want and need in a relationship or situation, and whether the people you're spending time with align with those values.

Remember that you don't have to settle for less than you deserve. Sometimes, people may try to convince us that we should be grateful for what we have, even if it's not what we truly want or need. But you deserve to be treated with respect and kindness, and as I mentioned before, it's okay to walk away from a situation or relationship that doesn't reflect that.

By shifting your perspective and focusing on what you want and need, you take control of your own happiness and ensure that you're surrounded by people who are good enough for you, who truly value and appreciate you.

THE TRUTH IS, YOU VALUE
OTHERS' OPINIONS MORE THAN
YOUR OWN. STOP IT!

○

HOW OTHERS SEE YOU IS
NOT IMPORTANT; HOW YOU SEE
YOURSELF IS EVERYTHING.

○

IF EVERYONE LIKES YOU,
YOU HAVE A SERIOUS PROBLEM!

○

STOP ALLOWING THE LIMITATIONS
OF THOSE AROUND YOU
TO BECOME YOUR OWN.

STOP EXPECTING ANYTHING LESS THAN YOU DESERVE:

REMEMBER,
YOU TEACH PEOPLE HOW TO TREAT YOU.

SELF-CARE SAVAGE WISDOM

It's easy to fall into the trap of settling for less than you deserve, but you have to remember that you are worthy of love, respect, and happiness. Learn to set boundaries and communicate your needs and wants clearly to those around you. By doing so, you are teaching people how to treat you and what you will and will not tolerate. If you don't speak up for yourself, others may not know what you expect from them.

Start being selective about whom you surround yourself with. It's okay to distance yourself from people who don't treat you well or who bring negativity into your life. You deserve to be surrounded by people who lift you up and make you feel good about yourself.

You can't control how other people treat you, but you can control how you react to it. If someone treats you badly consistently, it's up to you to set boundaries with them. If they still don't change their behavior even after communicating your needs, then you can decide whether to continue allowing this person into your life. You have the power to decide who or what you let into your life and what you are or are not okay with.

Do things that bring you joy and cultivate relationships with people who bring you good vibes. Don't settle for anything less than happiness. You deserve it!

THE MOMENT EVERYTHING
CHANGES IS WHEN YOU REALIZE
YOU DESERVE SO MUCH BETTER.

ALWAYS REMEMBER, YOU'RE WAY
TOO GOOD FOR SOMEONE WHO
ISN'T SURE ABOUT YOU.

YOU CAN'T MAKE SOMEONE
LOVE YOU BY GIVING THEM
MORE OF WHAT THEY ALREADY
DON'T APPRECIATE.

THE KILLER *OF ALL JOY*
IS COMPARISON.

Comparison is often cited as a major source of negative emotions, such as jealousy, envy, and low self-esteem. When you compare yourself to others, you tend to focus on what you lack or what you perceive as shortcomings in yourself, rather than appreciating your own distinctive qualities. This can lead to feelings of inadequacy and dissatisfaction in your own life.

Comparison can also be harmful in social situations, as it can lead to feelings of rivalry and competition, rather than cooperation and support. When you compare yourself to others, you may feel the need to compete with them or put them down in order to make yourself feel better. This can damage relationships and create a negative and competitive environment.

Comparing yourself to others makes it hard to enjoy things for what they are. For example, if you're at a concert but you are constantly comparing yourself to others, you may not be able to fully appreciate the music or the moment.

People often compare themselves to an idealized version of others, rather than the reality. Social media provides the perfect platform for this type of comparison. When you compare yourself to the idealized versions of others, you set yourself up for disappointment.

Don't let comparison destroy your joy. Celebrate your own strengths and skills.

WHAT OTHERS THINK OF YOU

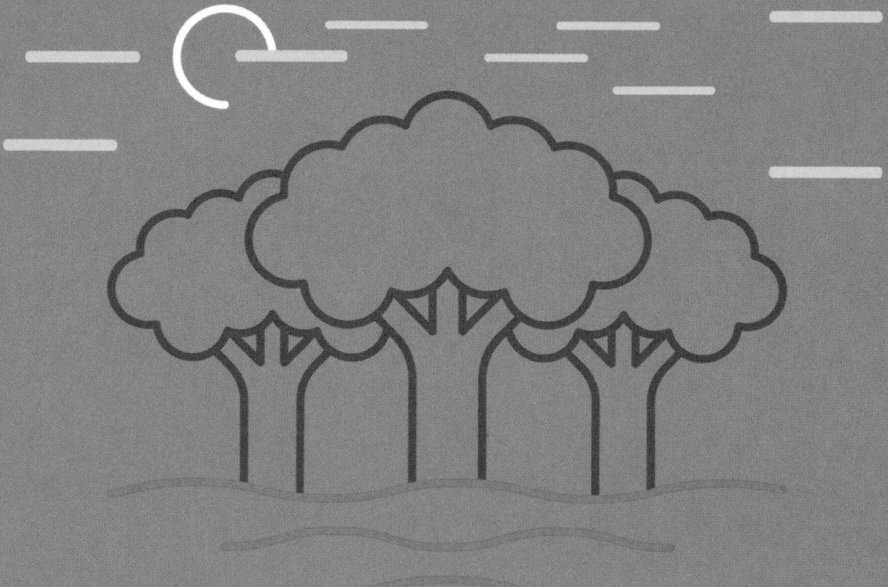

IS NONE OF YOUR BUSINESS!

People are going to think and perceive you as they do, and most of the time you're guessing what that perception is. Remember to focus on your own actions and attitude, rather than worrying about the opinions of others. This will encourage you to take responsibility for your own happiness and well-being, rather than seeking validation or approval from others.

By not being concerned with others' thoughts and opinions, you can live a more authentic, happy, and peaceful life, unencumbered by the constant need for validation and acceptance. It also frees up your mental energy that can be channeled toward more productive activities.

Trying to control or change others' opinions of you is often futile and can lead to frustration and disappointment. Everyone has their own unique perspectives and experiences, and therefore may have different opinions and perceptions of you.

Your own self-worth cannot be determined by what others think of you. It is determined by how you see yourself and how you live your life. Concentrate on your own growth and strengthening your own self-worth—then and only then will you stop trying to please or impress others.

Not everyone's opinion matters. Surround yourself with people who will be uplifting rather than those who are negative and critical. People's opinions are not always accurate or fair, and it is not always necessary to take them to heart.

Stop the futile and draining pursuit of what others think of you and stay focused on your own actions, attitude, and well-being.

CHAPTER 5

DARE TO FAIL AND PROTECT YOUR PEACE

When you become a Self-Care Savage
and do the work to heal and forgive,
growing a high self-worth, you'll feel a
peace and happiness in your life that you
may have never felt before and you'll
become a fierce protector of
this new peace.

The world will constantly try to steal your peace. From the day you're dropped on Earth, all of society, including your family and friends, will tell you how to live your life according to them, and if you don't, you will be criticized and judged. The reason is because the same thing was done to them, and most of all this guidance and advice is based on fear. Most people are afraid to fail even though failing is our best teacher. People are afraid to fail because society teaches us that there is only one way: success. And if we don't have it, whatever that means, then we have failed, and if we fail, then we aren't enough. And this story of not being enough keeps people in a place of fear, in a place where they can't see beyond the failure to the many possibilities that await them.

When life doesn't always turn out how we expect it to, we see it as a failure, but failure teaches us what we are made of and how powerful we truly are. We learn our best lessons when we fail at things. We are resilient and sometimes these redirections in life show us how strong we are. This is where you find out what you're made of.

When you fail at something that you thought you loved, such as a career or starting a business that you thought you wanted to get into, it can lead you in a different direction, a different opportunity that teaches you more about what passions truly make you happy. Our failures also teach us how to love and how to have compassion.

All of this is to say that you will fail at life sometimes, and that is okay. Life is all about failing, and without failure you probably would not be who you are right now.

SOMETIMES, WE HAVE TO GO THROUGH FAILURE TO GET TO WHERE WE ARE MEANT TO GO.

We usually have to go through a lot of pain and hurt before we wake up and take our lives back so we can find our peaceful selves. It's never too late in life and never too early to Self-Care Savage Up, do the work, and find some peace. I was fifty-two when I first felt some calmness and peace in my life. There is no age limit on when we can start to change our lives. You can still have peace, and it is your job to protect your peace.

Keeping your peace is about protecting yourself from these unmeasurable standards set by others and staying true to you. It means that even when people try to scare you into thinking that you have failed, that you will still keep moving toward peace. When you start to feel yourself getting back into your old patterns, know that this new you, this more healed you, this more peaceful you is worth protecting.

Some people will not support you or the way you want to live your life. There will be people in your life who don't deserve you, who will bring you down and not see your worth, and who will make you feel like you are not good enough—this is when you have to decide to protect your peace. This is when you have decide to let go of people and things that are not doing you well.

There will be people that you encounter in your quest who will not like you, and that's okay. You don't have to be liked by everybody to live the life you want and not everyone has to approve or understand the life you are living—that doesn't mean you have failed. Protecting your peace is about not worrying about what others think of you or whether they like you. It's about valuing yourself enough to know when it's time to live the life you want despite those around you or those limiting beliefs. It's about not wasting your time with people who can't see your worth or won't pour into you. It's about living life they way you want without letting the opinions of others define your journey.

When things don't go your way, a confident and healed you will start to see this as a redirection rather than something to run away from.

Bravery is facing the unknown, and when we fail at something we are entering a stage of uncertainty. We may not know the end result, but we are going to go forth on this amazing path anyway because we believe in ourselves so much that we know we will come out the other side better than before.

We aren't created to live stressed, angry, and scared lives. On the contrary, we were all put on this Earth to live a life full of purpose. We need to fail at things to find what we are looking for. And sometimes, our failures can break our hearts and happen at the worst possible time, but our failures help us overcome our deepest fears. And when we can face our fears, we can start to live the life we are meant to. And when we are In a place of complete serenity, there is no one who can take that away from us. Of course, there will be people and circumstances that will try, but don't let them take you away from the peace you have cultivated.

When you become a Self-Care Savage, you will have a different attachment to your peace and you won't let anybody take it from you.

The Friendly Reminders in this chapter will unlock some tools to help you protect your newfound peace. Go through these when you need to remind yourself of this precious thing worth protecting—your peace.

IT'S OKAY
TO LIVE A LIFE THAT
OTHERS DON'T UNDERSTAND.

It is perfectly normal and acceptable to live a life that others may not understand. Everyone is unique and has their own perspective, values, and goals. What may be important to one person may not be important to another. Protect your peace by living a life that is true to you, a life that is outside of others' expectations.

It can be challenging to navigate the expectations and opinions of others, but you are the only person who truly knows what is best for you. It is easy for others to project their own beliefs and values onto you, but ultimately, it is your life, and you have the right to make your own choices.

People are often more understanding and accepting than we give them credit for. Many people have gone through similar experiences and can relate to your choices, even if they may not fully understand them.

People who criticize or don't understand your choices are coming from a place of fear or insecurity. They may feel inadequate if you're doing more than them or if you're doing what makes you happy and they're not. They might be projecting their own fears or doubts onto you, or they might be so convinced that their way is the only way that they can't understand why you would want to live differently.

Self-Care Savage Up and protect your peace by not letting the opinions of others dictate how you live your life. Don't let the judgment or fears of others keep you from living purposefully, and living a life that intentionally aligns with your personal beliefs and aspirations.

YOU DO TOO MUCH EXPLAINING;
LET OTHERS THINK WHATEVER
THEY WANT AND MOVE ON!

IF THEY BRING YOU DOWN,
DON'T BRING THEM AROUND!

THE ONLY THING THAT'S WRONG WITH
YOU IS YOUR BELIEF THAT THERE IS
SOMETHING WRONG WITH YOU.

YOUR PEACE IS MORE IMPORTANT
THAN PROVING YOUR POINT.

IF YOU TRY AND FAIL, CONGRATULATIONS!

MOST PEOPLE DON'T EVEN TRY!

Trying and failing is a natural part of the learning and growth process. It is through trying and failing that we learn valuable lessons and gain the experience necessary to succeed in the future. The fact that you have attempted something, regardless of the outcome, is something to be proud of. It takes courage and determination to put yourself out there and try, and not everyone is willing to take that risk.

Failure is not the opposite of success, but rather a stepping-stone to it. Successful people are not immune to failure; they simply view it as a necessary part of the process. They understand that failure is not a reflection of their self-worth as a person, but rather a learning opportunity.

Also, failure is not final. Failure is not a dead end, but rather a fork in the road. When we fail, we have the opportunity to reevaluate our approach, learn from our mistakes, and come back stronger. Failure is not the end, but rather the beginning of a new journey.

Failure is not a measure of your ability, either. Some of the most successful people in the world failed numerous times before they succeeded. Failure is a sign of trying and taking risks; it's a sign of progress.

The most successful people are those who are able to learn from their failures and use them to their advantage to improve their skills, knowledge, and abilities. It is through trying and failing that we ultimately achieve success.

DON'T ASK PEOPLE FOR ADVICE WHO
HAVE NOT BEEN THERE, DONE THAT,
OR ARE DOING IT. IT'S A TIME WASTER.

IF YOU'RE NOT WILLING TO GET IT
WRONG, YOU'LL NEVER GET IT RIGHT!

SOMETIMES YOU NEED THINGS TO
GO WRONG, SO YOU CAN GET BACK
TO FOCUSING ON YOURSELF.

STOP WANTING

WHAT YOU DESERVE

FROM
PEOPLE WHO
WON'T OR
CAN'T

GIVE IT TO YOU.

It is important to set realistic expectations for the relationships and interactions we have with others. Not everyone is capable of giving the level of support, understanding, or commitment that you may desire or feel you deserve. Holding on to the belief that others should meet your expectations can lead to disappointment and resentment.

It can be helpful to take a step back and evaluate the dynamics of your relationships. Are there certain individuals who consistently fail to meet your needs or treat you in a way you don't want to be treated? If so, it may be necessary to reevaluate these relationships and consider limiting or ending them.

We can love someone, but if they aren't willing or able to love us back, then we have to make the decision to choose ourselves first. Know when to walk away from people who are giving you less than what you need. Everyone is at different stages in life—what you may be ready to give someone they may not be ready to give back to you. That doesn't necessarily make the other person bad, but sometimes you have to do what is best for you and protect this sacred contentment and self-love that you are creating for yourself.

Protect your peace and build a strong support system of people who do treat you with the respect and understanding you deserve. Work on becoming the best version of yourself, so that you can become more confident and self-assured and less reliant on the validation of others.

IF IT DOESN'T BRING YOU PEACE,
HAPPINESS, OR PURPOSE, THEN IT GETS
NO TIME, ENERGY, OR ATTENTION.

THERE'S A DIFFERENCE BETWEEN
PEOPLE WHO SEE YOU IN THEIR
FREE TIME AND THOSE WHO
FREE THEIR TIME TO SEE YOU.

WHEN SOMEONE GHOSTS YOU,
PROTECT YOUR PEACE, RESPECT
THE DEAD, AND MOVE ON.

CHASE PEACE INSTEAD OF PEOPLE!

PEOPLE DON'T HAVE TO LIKE YOU,

AND YOU DON'T HAVE TO CARE.

It is true that not everyone will like you, and that is perfectly okay. Everyone has their own preferences and opinions, and just because someone doesn't like you, it doesn't mean there is something wrong with you as a person. It is not necessary for everyone to like you in order for you to be fulfilled. Part of protecting your peace means not letting the opinions of others have an influence on your self-worth or your decisions.

Self-Care Savage Up and stop trying to make everyone like you. Trying to please everyone is a time waster mainly because it's never going to happen—there will always be someone who doesn't like you. Instead, focus on being true to yourself. When you are true to yourself, you will attract people who appreciate and respect you for who you are.

Rejection and criticism are a natural part of life. They can be difficult to deal with, but they can also be valuable opportunities for growth and learning. Instead of getting bogged down by negative opinions, try to learn from them and use them as motivation to improve yourself.

It's not necessary for everyone to like you, and you do not have to care if they do or don't or worry about what others think. By accepting that not everyone will like you and not caring about it, you will be able to cultivate a more peaceful mind-set and life.

STOP WORRYING ABOUT PEOPLE
WHO AREN'T WORRIED ABOUT YOU!

○

STOP TRYING TO BE LIKED
BY EVERYBODY, YOU DON'T EVEN
LIKE EVERYBODY!

○

SOME PEOPLE ARE INVESTMENTS,
AND A LOT OF PEOPLE ARE BILLS;
LEARN THE DIFFERENCE!

IF PEOPLE AREN'T LISTENING TO YOU,

STOP TALKING TO THEM.

When we communicate with others, it is integral that we are heard and understood. People who take the time to actively hear and understand us at least most of the time genuinely care about us and what we have to say.

If people are not listening to you, stop talking to them and figure out whether your relationship is important and whether they value you.

Someone may not be listening to you for a number of reasons: they may not be interested in the topic, or they may not trust or respect you, or they may not be in a position to listen and take action. If the relationship is important to you, then it may be best to find ways to reengage them in a more effective manner, whether that means finding a more interesting topic, building trust and respect before continuing the conversation, or waiting for a more appropriate time to have the conversation.

If the person has a tendency of not treating you well or they don't seem to value you as a loved one, then it may be best to reconsider talking to them at all.

Sometimes when we are not being heard, we can feel as if what we have to say is not important or worthy, which then affects the way we feel about ourselves. Just know that, sometimes, it may not be personal—that person may just not be ready to hear what you have to say. And if it is personal, as I said before, it is not your job to care what others think of you. It is your job to protect your peace by knowing when to stop talking to people who aren't listening.

NOTHING BRINGS YOU GREATER PEACE

THAN MINDING YOUR OWN DAMN BUSINESS!

When you focus on your own goals and responsibilities, you are less likely to become bogged down and distracted by the problems and issues of others. This can help you feel more in control of your life and less stressed and anxious. By minding your own business, you can improve your relationships with others, as you are less likely to be pulled into conflicts or drama.

When you are constantly worried about the problems and issues of others, it can be easy to lose sight of what is truly important to you. By focusing on your own priorities, you gain a sense of direction and purpose in your life. This can lead to greater satisfaction and fulfillment, as well as a sense of inner peace.

When you are constantly involved in the problems and issues of others, it can be difficult to maintain healthy and positive boundaries. By focusing on your own needs and goals, you can create more space in your life for positive interactions with others. This can lead to stronger, more supportive relationships, which can bring greater peace and happiness to your life.

Also note that minding your own business doesn't mean being indifferent to the needs of others, but rather to not become overly involved in their problems and issues unless it's necessary. Be aware of the balance between minding your own business and being supportive of others.

So, secure your peace and learn to mind your business.

CHAPTER 6

THE ONLY MOMENT THAT MATTERS

Living in the past and worrying
about the future. Sound familiar?
It does to me. I became an expert at this
in-between space. I was proficient in floating
between the past and the future, never quite
touching the present. I was too focused on
my past and so worried about my future
that I never appreciated the moment right
in front of me. This is how most people
navigate through life.

People often make decisions based on their past unhealed traumas and future worries that haven't even happened yet. Instead, reflect back and revisit a lesson when needed or to heal a wound, but don't ruminate in the same old hurtful thoughts. The thing about the past is that there are wounds that will never completely heal. And these deep wounds often creep up into our behaviors, feelings, and actions. They keep us from being happy and feeling like we deserve happiness.

Sometimes, the past can also keep us from experiencing any good in our current lives. If you keep holding on to the past, you will not be able to give yourself the moment you have now. The moment to change your life for the better. The moment to make a decision to Self-Care Savage Up and do the work that needs to be done so some goodness can come into your present.

Our past experiences make us who we are. A lot of us live with past guilt, hurt, or pain that is not ours to carry. Some people give this pain to us and some of us feel like we caused it. However, we can't change what has happened; we can only change what is currently happening right now. It's not easy to look beyond the past and move toward change, but the least you can do is try. All it takes is one decision, one moment, one simple step to start moving toward something better.

Worrying about the future is a big fat time waster. It kills your energy, creates a low mood, paralyzes you from being proactive on goals and opportunities, and takes away present-moment joys. The future is always uncertain. We don't know what will happen in the next five years, let alone the next few weeks, days, or even minutes. We can plan what we want to happen, but it doesn't always turn out the way we expect it to. While it's great to have a plan, it's also okay that something unexpected happens. Yes, it is scary, and yes, the unexpected is not always great. There will be circumstances and experiences that we will never see coming and that will be hard to get through, but you can't let them take over your life. You can't let the fear of what may happen tomorrow keep you from living in today.

Tomorrow is not always promised, so take a moment to enjoy where you are right now. Whenever you feel yourself starting to get lost in your thoughts—in that tricky in between of the past and the future—look around and pin your eye on an object. It can be a tree or a flower or a spoon from your cabinet. Ask yourself: What does it look like? Feel like? Smell like? Do I hear anything? Get in tune with your five senses to bring yourself back to the present moment.

THE PRESENT IS THE ONLY THING THAT MATTERS.

The past has already happened, and the future has yet to come. The present is happening right now and it's the one thing you have control over. You can control what you do right now, right here, and nothing else. Start to cultivate this present moment mind-set and you will see your perspective on things begin to change for the better.

Accept that there are things that you have no control over and that you cannot change what has already happened. Accept who and where you are in this moment. Offer yourself some compassion, because you are human. Give yourself some forgiveness and some grace. And most of all, be thankful for something in your life right now even if it is just the simple act of breathing. Continue to be thankful every day, whether it's enjoying a cup of coffee or getting that dream job you wanted. Creating a habit around practicing gratitude can help you appreciate your every day. Cultivating gratitude helps keep you in the moment. Whether you say it to yourself or write it down, make a habit of noticing what you are thankful for today.

It's time to Self-Care Savage Up and take back control of your thoughts and emotions. Start healing your past hurts and pull yourself back from the future into having a present moment mind-set, which is where you find and cultivate gratefulness, acceptance, compassion, forgiveness, happiness, self-worth, and peace. You will start to feel more peaceful and see yourself and your world in a much better light.

The Friendly Reminders in this chapter will help keep you in a present mindfulness state. Whenever you start to feel yourself getting caught up in your past traumas or future worries, or both, use these Friendly Reminders to prompt you to focus on the present and what is right in front of you. And remember, everything that matters is happening right now.

IF YOU'RE
CONSTANTLY THINKING

YOUR HAPPINESS IS
SOMEWHERE ELSE,

IT WILL
NEVER BE
WHERE YOU ARE.

Happiness is a state of mind and a personal experience. It is not something that can be found externally, but rather something that can be cultivated within yourself. It is not something you decide to do tomorrow or in some distant future. It is something you do constantly in the little present moments.

Many people believe that happiness is located somewhere else and that it will be achieved once they reach a certain goal or attain certain things. However, this is a fallacy. Happiness is not something that can be found in a specific place or thing; it can only be found within yourself.

People tend to focus on what they do not have rather than what they do have. They believe that happiness will only come when they attain something they do not currently possess. This is a setup for failure and will lead straight to dissatisfaction and unhappiness. The key to happiness is to appreciate and be grateful for what you already have.

Happiness can never be found where you are not. It is a state of mind that can be cultivated within yourself by focusing on the present moment, appreciating what you already have, and not comparing yourself to others.

Self-Care Savage Up and be more grateful for today, right now, this moment!

STOP IMAGINING WHAT LIFE WOULD
BE LIKE IF YOU CHANGED SOMETHING
AND START IMAGINING WHAT IT
WOULD BE LIKE IF YOU DIDN'T.

YOU CAN HAVE EXCUSES
OR YOU CAN HAVE RESULTS,
BUT YOU CAN'T HAVE BOTH!

WHATEVER YOU'RE NOT CHANGING,
YOU'RE CHOOSING!

STOP LOOKING FOR HAPPINESS IN
THE SAME PLACE THAT YOU LOST IT.

RIGHT NOW,

THIS MOMENT

IS THE ONLY MOMENT
THAT MATTERS.

The present moment is often referred to as the "now" and is considered to be the only point in time that truly exists. The past and the future are only concepts in our minds, and we can only experience the present moment through our senses. The importance of living in the present moment is often emphasized in spiritual and philosophical teachings, as it can help reduce stress, increase mindfulness, and improve well-being.

Being present allows us to fully engage in the current moment, rather than dwelling on the past or worrying about the future. This can increase our appreciation of the world around us and lead to greater satisfaction in life.

Living in the present moment has helped me be more productive and efficient, as I am able to focus more on the task at hand rather than getting caught up in distractions or worries. It has also helped me be more present in my relationships, allowing me to fully listen and connect with others.

Being present can be challenging, as our minds are often preoccupied with thousands of thoughts, usually of our past or future. But by practicing mindfulness, we can increase our ability to stay present, and it can improve our overall quality of life.

YESTERDAY WAS HEAVY,
SO PUT IT DOWN.

WORRYING DOES NOT TAKE AWAY
TOMORROW'S TROUBLE, IT TAKES
AWAY TODAY'S PEACE!

START LISTENING WITH YOUR
EYES AND YOU'LL START SEEING
EVERYTHING YOU NEED TO HEAR.

WHAT YOU'RE
NOT WILLING
TO DO TODAY,

YOU'RE NOT GOING
TO DO TOMORROW.

So you procrastinate on the hard things, the things that will actually make you better, feel better, feel healthier, because they're hard, they're painful, so you make another decision to put it off. You always tell yourself you'll do it tomorrow, and the next day, and it never happens. If you're not willing to do something today, you will very likely continue to avoid or delay doing it in the future. It's a horrible cycle, especially when it comes to your mental health.

You need to Self-Care Savage Up to take action and start today, right now! You deserve better, and nobody can or will do the work for you.

Procrastination is a common problem for many people and can have negative effects on productivity and your overall well-being.

It is crucial to understand the underlying reasons for procrastination and address them directly. For example, if fear of failure is the root cause for you not taking action toward a healthier you, remind yourself that failure is a natural part of change and is not the end of the world. If lack of motivation is the issue, find ways to make the task more interesting or meaningful. All of this is easy to say, it's just hard to do!

The point is, whatever you keep putting off won't change unless you decide to take action. Don't wait until tomorrow to be better: make the decision today, in this moment.

WHEN YOU GET QUIET, THINGS THAT ARE
IMPORTANT TO YOU GET REALLY LOUD.

○

YOUR GREATEST SELF HAS BEEN
WAITING YOUR WHOLE LIFE, SO DON'T
LET IT WAIT ANY LONGER.

○

IF YOU'RE WAITING ON PEOPLE TO DO STUFF
WITH, YOU'LL NEVER DO ANYTHING.

○

FOCUS ON YOURSELF, NOT THE
WORLD AROUND YOU. FIGHT THE BATTLES
INSIDE FIRST, THEN WATCH THE
WORLD CHANGE AROUND YOU.

THE STRUGGLE WITH
BEING PRESENT
ENDS

WHEN GRATITUDE
BEGINS!

The act of focusing on the things you're thankful for requires you to be fully engaged in the here and now, rather than dwelling on the past or worrying about the future. By practicing gratitude, you train your mind to be more attuned to the blessings in your life, rather than fixating on what is lacking.

Gratitude has the power to shift your perspective, allowing you to see challenges and difficulties in a new light. Rather than seeing them as overwhelming obstacles, you can view them as opportunities for growth and learning. When we approach life with an attitude of thankfulness, we become more resilient in the face of hardship, and are better equipped to handle the ups and downs of life.

When you take time to reflect on the things that you are thankful for, you tap into a deep well of positivity that can fuel you throughout the day.

When you practice gratitude, it spreads to those around you and creates a sense of community and connection. When we express gratitude for the people in our lives, we strengthen our relationships and build bonds that will last a lifetime. By focusing on the good in our lives, we inspire others to do the same, and contribute to a culture of positivity and kindness.

So, if you are struggling with being present, try starting a gratitude practice today. It can be as simple as saying or thinking one small thing you are thankful for every day. Being thankful is the Self-Care Savage way!

THE BRIGHT SIDE IS YOU
GET TO CHOOSE TO LOOK
ON THE BRIGHT SIDE.

○

STOP MAKING HAPPINESS
SO DIFFICULT AND BEING
GRATEFUL SUCH A CHORE!

○

GRUDGES AREN'T A WASTE OF
YOUR TIME, THEY'RE A WASTE
OF YOUR HAPPINESS.

ALL THAT CRAP

YOU STAY UP LATE AT NIGHT WORRIED ABOUT,

MOST OF IT

AIN'T EVEN GOING TO HAPPEN!

Worrying about the future can be a source of stress and anxiety for many people. A lot of the things we worry about don't actually ever happen. It's important to find ways to manage it so that it doesn't take over your life. Instead of dwelling on potential negative outcomes, try to focus on what you can control in the present moment.

One effective way to stop worrying about the future is to practice mindfulness. Mindfulness means being present and aware in the moment, without judgment. There are many ways to practice mindfulness, such as through meditation, yoga, or simply paying attention to your breath.

By far the most effective approach Is to Self-Care Savage Up and incorporate the use of cognitive-behavioral therapy (CBT) to change the way you think about the future. CBT is a type of therapy that helps people identify and change negative thought patterns that contribute to anxiety and depression. By learning to identify and challenge negative thoughts, you can replace them with more positive, realistic thoughts. I use this technique hundreds of times a day. To find out more about (CBT), consult a cognitive-behavioral therapist or search online.

Engaging in nature by doing any kind of physical activity will help you stay in the now. When you are feeling physically and emotionally well, it can be easier to manage worries about the future.

THE PEACE
YOU HAVE NOW

IS WORTH
EVERYTHING
THAT YOU'VE LOST!

Sometimes in our quest for peace, we may lose things and people. All of the things that are not doing you any good will start to fall away as you continue on your own Self-Care Savage path. It won't be easy, and it often involves facing difficult emotions, memories, and experiences, as it did for me in my own journey. But in the end, the sense of calm and contentment that comes with finding Inner peace is truly priceless.

Doing the Self-Care Savage work helped me identify and work through my own personal issues and traumas—it only took ten years (ha, ha), but I got here, which allowed me to develop a deeper understanding and acceptance of who I am as a person.

I am now able to focus on the things that truly matter to me, without letting fears or insecurities about the future dominate my thoughts.

The journey may have been difficult, but it was also incredibly rewarding and empowering. And, I am grateful for the lessons and growth that came along with it.

You may lose friends or family members in this quest for peace, but you will also lose the need to stay stuck in the past and the things that pull you toward worrying about the future. You will gain a new appreciation of the present moment. You will be grateful for all that you have now and treasure your newfound sense of peace and healing. Just remember that whatever you have lost is worth the price of living a more peaceful life.

CHAPTER 7

LEAD BY EXAMPLE

Self-leadership first is what inspires others. To be better for others you have to be better for yourself first. You can't advise someone else to change their lives if you are not doing the work to improve your own life.

As I've been saying throughout this book, no one can lead your life for you. Nobody can or will do the work for you. Taking responsibility for your own life, your own actions, and your own emotions is what will bring purpose, peace, and happiness. Leadership begins with you. Only you can make the changes that need to happen in your reality. Only you have the power to decide to turn things around and only you get to decide what you want out of life. You are in charge of your destiny, so be the leader of your life story.

You can start stepping into this leadership mentality by making the commitment to doing the Self-Care Savage work that we have been discussing in the previous chapters. This includes taking care of yourself first, healing your wounds, forgiving yourself and others, growing your confidence, protecting your peace, and staying focused on the present moment. You have to be accountable for how your life is now as an adult to take charge of it and become the Self-Care Savage that you are meant to be.

ONCE YOU START TO TAKE THE LEAD IN YOUR OWN LIFE, THEN YOU CAN BE A LEADER FOR OTHERS AND INSPIRE OTHERS WITH YOUR STORY.

Sharing your journey of healing with others is all part of your own continued self-care. You don't have to become a great speaker, but it is definitely helpful if you want to spread a message. When you share your story, you inspire other people to do the Self-Care Savage work. You lead by example. You become someone that others look up to when they are having a hard time. Spread the message so that you can lead the world in love.

For me, wanting to lead by example was what inspired me to put myself out there on social media and create my "Friendly Reminder" videos. It did and continues to play a big part with my own therapy and is a surefire way to hold myself accountable with my own Self-Care Savage work. It is a way to lead myself, do the work, and become disciplined. I knew that by holding myself accountable in making the videos for others I was also holding myself accountable in continuing to do the work I needed to do to be a better me. I could not give other people advice without first following and doing the Self-Care Savage work myself.

I've always let the Friendly Reminder community know that I was speaking to myself first. My page has resonated and inspired millions of others to Self-Care Savage Up. My gratitude is through the roof. I truly believe that I get more from my followers watching my videos than making them. Everyone's supportive and encouraging comments have inspired me to levels I can't put into words yet.

You don't have to share as much as I do or how I do it, but I can tell you that just touching one person with your story can make a big difference in our world. And that person might do more for you in your continued Self-Care Savage work than you are able to do for them! Telling someone your story is a great way to keep yourself in check, to remember that you are still doing good work. Knowing that you can help change someone else's life by sharing your story will motivate you to keep going,

Sometimes that little push someone needs to start changing their life is your positive example. If someone doesn't believe they can change for the better because they haven't seen it happen or haven't heard someone in their life do it, then most likely they won't believe they can do it, too. Sharing your story helps people believe that they can heal, forgive, and take care of themselves as well. Share your story however you feel most comfortable doing it—whether you're just telling a close friend, telling your whole family, sharing on social media, or sharing anonymously through a blog.

And I want to also say that you don't have to share your story until you are ready to do so. Or, if you don't want to share your story, that's okay too. It's your story to share or not share, but know that you will be doing so much good to the world by sharing it, if you do choose to do so.

In today's world, nobody is listening; everybody is watching. Everyone has eyes on them from somebody else looking to see how they handle life. There's always someone looking up to you even when you don't know it. There are people that you probably look up to yourself and probably inspired you to start your own journey. You can be that person for someone else.

When life gets hard, just remember: you are an inspiration, you are a leader. You are a Self-Care Savage!

The Friendly Reminders in this chapter are some of my favorites to keep you on the Self-Care Savage path: healing, forgiving, knowing your worth, protecting your peace, and staying in a present mindful state to lead your own life by example!

THE LEVEL AT WHICH YOU LEAD YOURSELF

IS THE LEVEL AT WHICH YOU CAN LEAD OTHERS.

When you become a Self-Care Savage and work to better yourself, the following will just become part of who you are by default. In order to be an effective leader, you must first be able to lead yourself.

Leadership is not just about being in charge of others, but also about being able to inspire and guide them toward a common goal. A leader who is able to lead themselves effectively is more likely to be able to inspire and guide others in the same way.

Being self-disciplined and having a strong sense of self-awareness also allows a leader to be more adaptable and responsive to the needs of those they lead. Such leaders are able to recognize their own strengths and weaknesses and make adjustments accordingly.

A leader who is able to lead themselves effectively is able to set clear goals and work toward them with determination and focus. They understand the importance of persistence and hard work, and are not easily discouraged by setbacks or obstacles. They do the Self-Care Savage work, and it shows.

You can't lead others well if you have not led yourself well. It all starts with you, as you have most likely learned by now. You are the key for everything else in your life, and that includes leadership. When you choose to be a Self-Care Savage, you choose to be a leader for others in change. The best way to lead someone else through this Self-Care Savage Up journey is to lead yourself through it. A leader and a Self-Care Savage are the same thing!

THE REST OF THE WORLD CAN WAIT;
BE THE BEST FOR YOURSELF FIRST,
THEN GIVE THEM WHAT THEY HAVE
BEEN WAITING FOR!

THE WORK YOU DO ON
YOURSELF IS THE GIFT YOU
GIVE TO EVERYONE ELSE.

YOU'RE THE FUEL TO YOUR
HAPPINESS OR YOUR SADNESS!

THERE'S A DIFFERENCE BETWEEN
GIVING UP AND KNOWING WHEN
YOU'VE HAD ENOUGH.

ALWAYS BE UNAPOLOGETICALLY YOURSELF

AND LET OTHERS DO THE SAME!

Authenticity is crucial for being an effective leader, as it helps to build trust and credibility. When a leader is authentic, they are true to themselves and their values, which allows others to see and understand their motivations. This creates a positive and empowering environment, where everyone feels comfortable being themselves and expressing their own thoughts and ideas.

Authentic leaders also empower others to be authentic in their own right. By creating a culture of openness and transparency, they encourage others to share their own thoughts and ideas.

An authentic leader always demonstrates their values and principles through their actions. They also promote a culture of accountability and responsibility, where everyone is expected to take ownership of their actions and make decisions based on their own values and beliefs.

Authentic leaders are able to create strong, meaningful relationships with those that look to them for guidance. By being transparent and honest in their interactions, they build trust and respect. They also encourage open communication and feedback, which helps to build collaborative and supportive interactions.

People who are always unapologetically themselves and empower others to do the same lead by example, inspiring others to be their best selves. Authentic leaders are the black belts of Self- Care Savages.

Let's go!

WE ALL HAVE TWO LIVES, AND THE
SECOND ONE BEGINS WHEN YOU
REALIZE YOU'RE GOING TO RUN OUT
OF TIME ON THE FIRST ONE.

BE YOU ALWAYS;
THE WORLD WILL ADJUST!

THERE IS NO COURAGE IN TRYING
TO FIT IN, ONLY COURAGE IN
BEING EXACTLY WHO YOU ARE.

STOP ADAPTING

TO THE ENERGY AROUND YOU

AND START INFLUENCING

THE ENERGY THAT'S AROUND YOU!

It can be easy to fall into the trap of adapting to the energy around you, rather than actively shaping it to align with your goals and values. By taking an active role in influencing the energy around you, you can create a more positive and productive environment for yourself and others.

One way to start influencing the energy around you is by setting clear boundaries and communicating them effectively. As I mentioned earlier, this can mean saying no to requests or demands that do not align with your values or priorities and setting limits on the amount of time and energy you are willing to invest in certain relationships or activities. By clearly communicating your boundaries, you can ensure that others understand how you want to be treated and that you are not taken advantage of.

Another way to influence the energy around you is by actively seeking out positive and uplifting experiences. This can mean spending time with people who make you feel good, engaging in activities that make you happy, and surrounding yourself with things that bring you inspiration and motivation.

You can also influence the energy around you by being mindful of the energy you are putting out into the world. This can mean being aware of your thoughts, emotions, and actions and making sure they align with your values and goals. A Self-Care Savage by default brings positive energy to any environment they step into. Are you ready?

IF YOU WANT TO LIFT YOURSELF UP,
THEN LIFT SOMEONE ELSE UP.

○

YOUR GREATEST TEST WILL BE HOW YOU
HANDLE PEOPLE WHO MISHANDLE YOU!

○

STOP EXPECTING PEOPLE TO BE HAPPY
WITH YOU OR FOR YOU IF YOU CAN'T
EVEN BE HAPPY WITH YOURSELF.

○

IT'S BETTER TO BE ALONE THAN
WITH SOMEONE WHO MAKES
YOU FEEL ALONE.

THE
GREATEST GIFT
YOU CAN GIVE ANOTHER PERSON

IS YOUR OWN HAPPINESS.

When we are happy, we radiate positivity and good energy, which can have a positive impact on those around us. When we are happy, we tend to be more patient, understanding, and kind, which can help improve our relationships with others. Additionally, when we are happy, we tend to be more productive and successful in our personal and professional lives, which can inspire others to strive for similar success.

Being happy also means that we are better equipped to handle difficult situations and challenges that may arise. When we are in a positive state of mind, we tend to be more resilient and better able to cope with stress and adversity. This can be especially important in helping others overcome their own struggles.

Happiness is also a state of mind that can be cultivated and nurtured through various practices, such as mindfulness, gratitude, and positive thinking. By taking the time to actively work on our own happiness, we not only improve our own lives, but we also have the power to spread positivity to the people around us. This is what Self-Care Savages do!

You are a bigger influence than you think. There is someone looking up to you, and the greatest gift you can give them is being happy. When you show someone that happiness is achievable, they want a piece of it too and want to try to find it for themselves. And as I explained earlier, when you do the work to be better, you will be better for others!

YOU CAN'T FORCE PEOPLE
TO SEE YOUR AWESOMENESS,
YOU'RE JUST GOING TO HAVE TO
LET THEM MISS OUT.

○

STOP EXPECTING IT TO BE EASY,
THEN IT WILL BE EASY!

○

ATTITUDE IS FREE!

IF YOU'RE
LUCKY ENOUGH
TO BE DIFFERENT,

DON'T CHANGE!

SELF-CARE SAVAGE WISDOM

Real leaders welcome their differences as strengths. They are Self-Care Savages doing the work to lead by example. Being different can be a valuable asset in life. There is no one "right" way to be, and different perspectives and experiences can bring new and valuable ideas to the table.

When you try to conform to societal norms or fit in with a certain group, you may be sacrificing the qualities that make you special. By staying true to yourself, you can build a sense of self-confidence and self-worth that will serve you well in all areas of your life. You can also lead people in doing the same—in accepting who they are and embracing the qualities that make them unique.

Many people struggle with self-doubt or insecurity about their differences, and a kind word or gesture of support can make a big difference.

Being different is what makes the world more vivid and exciting. If everyone were the same, I don't think there would be anything interesting to look forward to. Being different can be challenging, but embracing who you are and standing up for yourself can help you overcome obstacles and lead you closer to your goals.

It is important to remember that being different is not something to be ashamed of, but rather something to be celebrated. Self-Care Savage Up knowing that being different makes a difference!

The way in which something is said can be just as important as the words themselves. The tone, inflection, facial expressions, and body language you use can greatly affect how your message is received. For example, if you say "I'm fine" in a flat, monotone voice, with a mean look on your face, it is likely that the listener will not believe you and will think you are not actually fine. On the other hand, if you say the same words with a cheerful tone and smile, the listener will likely believe that you are indeed fine.

The way in which you deliver a message can also affect the listener's perception of you. If you are consistently rude and dismissive in your communication, the listener is likely to view you as arrogant and unapproachable. On the other hand, if you are consistently polite and respectful in your communication, the listener is likely to view you as kind and approachable.

It's also important to consider the context of your communication. If you are delivering a presentation to a group of people, the way in which you deliver the information will greatly affect how well it is received. Tone, inflection, body language, nonverbal communication, and context are all important factors to consider when communicating with others.

Being aware of these factors can help ensure that your message is received the way you intend it to be. Being a great communicator makes for a powerful leader.

THANK YOU

Thank you to Rage Kindelsperger, VP, Group Publishing Director at Quarto, for being a Friendly Reminder supporter and believing the book could benefit more people all over the world.

Thank you to my editor, Keyla Pizarro-Hernández, for making me look like an author, haha.

Thank you to the UCan Outdoors/ Friendly Reminder community for all the involvement, encouragement, and support ya'll continue to provide every day. That's what made this book possible.

And a very special thank you to all the content creators willing to put their healing on display through social media; you are leading by example and saving lives!

ABOUT THE AUTHOR

Scott Tatum is a father, nomad, hiker, and explorer traveling full-time supporting our public lands and advocating for mental health.

Scott utilizes the outdoors for his own form of therapy, healing the mind, body, and soul. This has led Scott to creating a platform through social media to deliver powerful messages that bring a whole new spin to the ideas of self-care and healing. He believes that you're always one decision away from a totally different life.

Each week, Scott delivers "Friendly Reminders" via his social media channels to help millions of others realize the power of self-care first, self-worth, mindfulness, and self-awareness. Scott is a self-professed "Self-Care Savage," being fiercely committed to his self-care and knowing that doing the work on yourself every day makes you better for yourself so you can be better for others. You can't pour from an empty cup.

From his Friendly Reminders, Scott reminds us that self-care and taking accountability for your own self-growth are vital to well-being. You can follow Scott and catch his impactful Friendly Reminders at @ucanoutdoors on all social media platforms.